STAY CALM
WITH SENECA

Jana Capri lives in Barcelona, Spain, speaks five languages and holds a degree in Translation and Interpretation from Charles University in Prague. She is a Master Practitioner in NLP (Neuro-Linguistic Programming) and has studied psychological astrology and creative writing. Jana is also a blogger and co-author of several books.

She has a strong interest in psychosomatics and personal growth and enjoys reading and writing books that inspire self-improvement and help others feel better about themselves.

Charan Díaz Arquillo is a psychologist based in Barcelona, Spain, with over twenty years of experience in psychotherapy, personal growth, educational psychology and organisational psychology. He holds a master's degree in Humanistic and Integrative Psychotherapy, as well as certifications in Mindfulness and Clinical Hypnosis from the University of Barcelona. Charan is also an author and co-author of several books.

He is passionate about Hindu and Greek philosophy, as well as oriental tales and mythology.

JANA CAPRI AND CHARAN DÍAZ

STAY CALM

WITH SENECA

79 QUESTIONS AND ANSWERS FROM STOIC PHILOSOPHY

Published by Westland Books, a division of Nasadiya Technologies Private Limited, in 2025

No. 269/2B, First Floor, 'Irai Arul', Vimalraj Street, Nethaji Nagar, Alapakkam Main Road, Maduravoyal, Chennai 600095

Westland and the Westland logo are the trademarks of Nasadiya Technologies Private Limited, or its affiliates.

This English edition for the Indian Subcontinent published by arrangement with Suasive Consultants Private Limited (www.montsecortazar.com).

ISBN: 9789360456627

10 9 8 7 6 5 4

Typeset by Jojy Philip

Printed at Thomson Press India Private Limited

CONTENTS

INTRODUCTION

A crust eaten in peace is better than a banquet partaken in anxiety.

—Aesop

Human beings have, without a doubt, spectacular potential. No other living being on our planet has managed to walk on the moon, write poetry or create vaccines that can save millions of lives. But there is one life that no vaccine or other scientific breakthrough can save: our inner life.

We suffer as much from anxiety today as we did two thousand years ago. In those times, human beings already worried about issues such as pleasing others, unfulfilled expectations, problems with difficult people, fear of death, financial troubles, the passage of time, the meaning of life or spiritual confusion. The worries that caused us such anxiety were similar to those that make us suffer today and, in essence, are probably the same ones that will cause us to suffer anxiety in the future.

How can Lucius Annaeus Seneca, who was born in Córdoba, Spain, in 4 BCE and was a contemporary of Jesus, help us with the type of anxiety we experience here and now?

Seneca, as a good Roman Stoic philosopher, sought to alleviate human mental suffering by devoting his whole life to a practical philosophy that deals with the great issues of human existence. And since our inner world has not changed much, Seneca's Stoic philosophy, which was useful then to assuage the anxiety of such concerns, is also useful today in our modern world.

In psychotherapy, to defuse unhealthy anxiety, it is useful to identify the 'hidden irrational beliefs' in our way of seeing something, and then to come up with an 'improved' and healthier version of those thoughts.

Well, a similar scheme is the one we will follow in this work, with a format or style of dialogue with questions and answers between a seeker (of truth) and Seneca, where the philosopher always improves or broadens the point of view of anxiety, alleviating it and relativising the problem with his answers.

All of Seneca's answers are inspired by his original quoted work. The answers are not always verbatim quotations, but are adapted to improve the reader's understanding for today's world. In a dialogue format with his interlocutor, the philosopher comes alive before the reader and makes it easier to learn from him, identify with the conversation and to remember his wisdom for the future.

We wish you a happy psychological–philosophical journey, where you will feel less anxiety in Seneca's company and, if at least one of his ideas helps you to obtain greater serenity at some point in your existence, then the time and attention devoted to this book will have been worth it.

HOW TO USE THIS BOOK

On the next page we explain the three parts of each chapter: (1) a seeker's question or comment, (2) Seneca's answer and (3) a psychological reflection.

By 'seeker' we mean all those who ask themselves questions about the mysteries of life and want to get answers based on this everlasting wisdom.

Seneca's answers are inspired by his work *Moral Letters to Lucilius*, specially selected to deal with anxiety and adapted to modern language for easy understanding.

The subsequent psychological reflection is food for thought, aiming to guide further reflection on Seneca's messages. These suggested reflections should not be considered instructions or definitive interpretations of the Stoic messages, but rather invitations for the reader to pose questions and to consider elements that might help to integrate the Stoic approach into their life.

1

FOCUS ON THE REAL DANGER

Question/comment from a seeker:

When I think of all the bad things that can happen to me, I get very afraid.

Seneca's answer (letter 5):

Animals just get scared and run away in the face of a real danger and then relax.

What is the point of you suffering unnecessarily for the past or the future if you do not respond to a real danger?

Psychological Reflection

Anxiety is closely related to anticipating in our imagination the worst that can happen.

Imagine that from now on, every time you have to make a decision, your mind is saturated with catastrophic thoughts. Would you be able to stay calm, move forward and be productive?

In that sense, it is useful to observe and learn from the stress of animals and worry only as long as we are faced with a real present danger. We do not live in a dangerous jungle. So, let's try to switch off, enjoy and relax whenever possible.

Question or comment on life.

Seneca's answer to anxiety inspired by his work *Moral Letters to Lucilius*. The reference to the corresponding letter is in brackets.

Psychological reflection to explore the message in more depth.

HOW TO GET THE MOST OUT OF THIS BOOK

We recommend that you use this book whenever:

- You are going through a difficult period in your life.
- You want to reduce your anxiety level.
- You need more peace of mind.
- You want to relieve worries, stress, etc.
- You are looking for inspiration.

You can select from the index the chapter name that inspires you most, or open the book randomly and see which message you land upon.

The great sages and philosophers of human history such as Seneca, Marcus Aurelius, Socrates, Epictetus or Buddha help us to understand that cultivating the desired attitude is not a matter of days, months or years, but a lifelong work.

Despite this, it is worth the effort.

1

FOCUS ON THE REAL DANGER

Question/comment from a seeker:

When I think of all the bad things that can happen to me, I get very afraid.

Seneca's answer (letter 5):

Animals just get scared and run away in the face of a real danger and then relax.

What is the point of you suffering unnecessarily for the past or the future if you do not respond to a real danger?

Psychological Reflection

Anxiety is closely related to anticipating in our imagination the worst that can happen.

Imagine that from now on, every time you have to make a decision, your mind is saturated with catastrophic thoughts. Would you be able to stay calm, move forward and be productive?

In that sense, it is useful to observe and learn from the stress of animals and worry only as long as we are faced with a real present danger. We do not live in a dangerous jungle. So, let's try to switch off, enjoy and relax whenever possible.

2

A BALANCED MIND

Question/comment from a seeker:

Lately, I have so many things on my mind that I can't even sleep. What can I do?

Seneca's answer (letter 2):

It is a sign of a balanced mind that you can be at ease with yourself wherever you are. You cannot feel good if your mind is in too many places at once.

Psychological Reflection

We seem to live in a constant rush, as if everything is urgent. Today's society seems to demand too much of us: jobs with endless working hours, partnerships, raising children, friendships, caring for parents, exercising our bodies, eating healthy, managing problems of all kinds, etc. And each of these expectations demands two very important things from us: our time and attention. We are always juggling our energy, time and attention with a whole host of things.

Multitasking and anxiety seem to be our daily bread and butter, especially in the workplace, where more and more demands are being placed on us. We have to be able to do all kinds of tasks quickly and, moreover, do many things at the same time. This is called being 'efficient', but we can also call it 'squeezing the orange to the very last drop'.

So it is completely normal that when it is time to rest, we don't always know how to stop the wheel that we have kept running at full speed all day long.

How is it possible that it is so difficult to rest when we are so tired? Could it be that we don't know how to switch off because we have lost the habit of doing so?

The Seneca philosophy encourages you to simplify your life, to prioritise, to find time for leisure and meditation. It encourages you to clean up your life, your time and your attention so that you don't go around like a headless chicken.

3

THE PRICE OF YOUR DESIRES

Question/comment from a seeker:

I want to have a house with my own swimming pool and garden, a luxury car and I am willing to work as much as it takes to afford the lifestyle I long for.

Seneca's answer (letter 42):

What is the price you really pay for what you want?
Often, the most valuable things are those that do not cost money. I could give you many examples of things that once bought or acquired deprive you of your freedom, and we would be freer if these things did not belong to us.

Both when it comes to acquiring things and when it comes to losses, think: 'It was a temporary thing'. That thing was alien to you and your existence when it came into your life, and without it you will live as easily as you did before you possessed it.

Psychological Reflection

What do you work for? To earn your salary, you give your time, your energy and your attention. That is the price you pay in order to get paid.

And it often happens that in order to have a higher level of income and to afford more things, you have to tip the scales and invest even more time and energy.

But if you tip the scales too far, what will happen? Will it be worth it? Will you continue to be a free person, or will you become a slave to your own desires?

Seneca tells us that everything has a cost. Therefore, it is important to make the right calculations and decide whether it is worth it to wear ourselves out, to waste our energy, our time and our life in exchange for whims that may demand a price too high. Or if, on the other hand, it is worth being more austere and modest in exchange for more freedom and peace of mind.

What is the price of your desires?

4

YOU NEVER LOSE WHAT IS YOURS

Question/comment from a seeker:

I have suffered a lot of losses lately. How can I be well when everything I love, I lose?

Seneca's answer (letter 9):

You will never lose what is truly yours. No one can take it away from you.

Whatever happens, all my assets will always be within me: my abilities, my values and my good judgement.

Psychological Reflection

An Asian proverb says: 'You only own what you cannot lose in a shipwreck'. If we apply this criterion, our house, money, parents or children do not really belong to us. They are temporary things, since we can lose them all.

But Seneca points out that we will never lose what is inside us, and that is where we must cultivate ourselves. Our faith, our values, our mental health, etc.—these belong to us to a greater extent, and lasts longer. There is nothing and nobody externally that can take these away from us without our consent.

5

LONELINESS

Question/comment from a seeker:

I can't stand loneliness; I always need to have people around me.

Seneca's answer (letter 6):

You will never be alone if you are your own friend. Hecaton said that he made progress when he started to be a good friend to himself. And that is the first step to being a good friend to others.

Psychological Reflection

What is loneliness? Can a wife sleep next to her husband, be with her children at home, but still feel lonely? And can someone with faith be lost in a desert with no one to keep themselves company and not feel lonely?

Seneca tells us that you will not be lonely if you treat yourself as a friend. The French philosopher Jean-Paul Sartre comes to a similar conclusion when he says: 'If you feel lonely when you are alone, you are in bad company'.

So, the starting point for feeling less lonely and being able to relate better to others is to know how to treat yourself well, as a friend would treat another friend.

Because if you can't stand yourself, how can you expect others to stand you?

6

WHAT PORT ARE YOU HEADING FOR?

Question/comment from a seeker:

What shall I do with my life? What is the most important thing? What should I take into account to enjoy a good life?

Seneca's answer (letter 71):

To know what is good to avoid and what is good to desire, raise your eyes, and remember the main purpose of your life. Only those whose actions are aligned with the highest purpose of their existence can have an orderly life.

No painter can achieve a good portrait unless he is clear about what he wants to paint, even if he has all the necessary colours at hand. Our mistake is that we do not reflect on the ultimate purpose of life; we are only concerned with certain moments of that life.

For those who do not know what port they are heading for, no wind will ever be favourable.

Psychological Reflection

We see the tree, but lose sight of the forest. We stress and worry—sometimes excessively—about some trees that we don't like, about things or episodes in life that are temporary.

But life is not a tree, it is a forest. It is a complex entity, and its meaning will be drawn by connecting many dots or different existential stages.

Let us broaden our search, let us reflect on what is the purpose of human life in general and ours in particular. As Seneca tells us, to get anywhere we must first know where we are going.

What is the main purpose of your life? Perhaps it is to learn to love, to learn to live, to be self-realised, to be happy, to perceive God or to reach absolute serenity.

Do you think it will help to remember what the whole meaning of your life is, in order to clear your mind the next time you are worried about a specific issue?

7

DON'T LOOK AT THE PEDESTAL

Question/comment from a seeker:

It makes me feel anxious to compare myself with people who are successful, those who don't have to worry about money, those who are famous . . .

Seneca's answer (letter 76):

Of all the rich, powerful and famous people, none of them have to be 'great people'.

Why do they seem so great and important to you then? Because you only look at their pedestal. But a dwarf at the top of a mountain is still a dwarf, and a giant at the bottom of a chasm is still a giant.

Thus, we make the mistake of valuing people by their appearance, status and material possessions, without seeing who that person truly is.

To discover who a person really is, widen your gaze, imagine them naked without their material possessions, without their status and without the rest of the deceptive illusions of fortune. Even forget about their body: look at their soul and its inclinations.

Psychological Reflection

In the age of social media, we are increasingly anxious to compare ourselves with those who claim to have the perfect life, the perfect partner, the perfect holiday. Deep down, we know that there is much more 'makeup' than 'natural beauty' beneath appearances. But sometimes we forget all that.

In Seneca's time, there were no photo filters or social networks, but there were people who appeared to be more than they really were and others who suffered when compared with them.

If you want to evaluate a person correctly, imagine them in a shipwreck, where they have lost everything and find themselves without possessions or positions, without any status or power. Would their personality, their company and their manner be pleasant? How would they strive to achieve their goals and satisfy their needs? Would they be shallow or deep and caring? What kind of person would they really be?

When you stop looking at the 'pedestal', you will get a more realistic picture of others and this will help you have a better image of yourself.

8

HOW TO COPE BETTER WITH ILLNESS

Question/comment from a seeker:

I'm scared of getting sick.

Seneca's answer (letter 78):

There are three reasons for fearing an illness: fear of death, pain in the body and the loss of pleasures.

1) What really scares us about death is how life works. You will die anyway because dying is part of life (and not because you have become ill). When you avoid illness, your health improves. But that doesn't free you from death anyway.
2) There is a limit to the body's pain, and when we suffer there are also pain-free intervals. Nature has made it

possible to experience only brief or tolerable pain up to a limit.

3) And as for giving up certain pleasures in illness, although it may be difficult at first, when you have experienced this routine for a while, you will desire them less and less, and you will reach a point where you no longer need them.

Psychological Reflection

Illness is part of life and beyond our control. But we can control the anxiety we feel when we think about it.

Seneca's proposal is to see illness from a point of view that alleviates the fear we feel towards it. If we learn to perceive it with less drama, we will suffer less and gain serenity.

Just as drugs relieve physical pain, there are psychological exercises related to the control of mental attention that can help to regulate physical and emotional pain (search for clinical hypnosis and pain, or mindfulness and pain).

How does Seneca's reflection help you to control your fear of getting sick? What could you think or do to take it more philosophically?

9

ACT LIKE A GLADIATOR

Question/comment from a seeker:

I always try to be well prepared for everything, but when I don't manage to prepare and something takes me by surprise, I get very nervous.

Seneca's answer (letter 22):

An old proverb says: 'It is in the arena that the gladiator decides how to fight.'

Until the gladiator has the opponent in front of him, observes his face, how he moves, and so forth, he cannot choose the most effective strategy for success.

No one can prepare one hundred per cent for a situation without being in it. It is in the action of the real situation that you will see best what you need to do.

Psychological Reflection

Seneca tells us that sometimes you have to 'dive into the pool' to learn to swim. This message is especially useful for people who think too much before they act. His metaphor of the gladiator who, only in the action of the fight, identifies the most effective resources he needs to win illustrates that sometimes we understand a situation only when we decide to step forward.

If you are worried about being in a situation without sufficient prior preparation, remember this metaphor of Seneca's gladiator to calm and protect your mind from useless anticipatory stress.

It also helps to take things in small doses that you can handle to normalise the situation and see that it is not as serious as it seems—that you have more resources than you think.

10

THE SERENE PERSON

Question/comment from a seeker:

What qualities does a serene person have?

Seneca's answer (letter 76):

The mature person accepts divine will, without being frustrated by unexpected problems or lamenting their own fate. They accept what life offers them and adapt to it with patience.

If our focus is not on our inner values and maturity, we will be weak and suffer from the changing fortunes of life.

Psychological Reflection

'If you want to make God laugh, tell him your plans,' a Jewish proverb tells us.

We do not know the future, and sometimes life brings us to a point where our plans go awry. The whole world has witnessed in the year 2020 how everyone's plans and expectations have had to be rethought with the emergence of the COVID-19 pandemic. It is a radical example of the human need to be mentally able to adapt and keep our composure and our values in the face of unexpected and desperate situations.

If we want to gain serenity, according to Seneca, we must first accept that we do not control everything. We may call it fate, divine will, or chance, but there is something beyond our control that pulls the strings and continually demands our acceptance, humility and adaptability to move forward without losing our heads or becoming disheartened.

11

REMOVE THE MASK

Question/comment from a seeker:

Lately, I think my life is full of misfortunes.

Seneca's answer (letter 24):

Try to see the situation in a more objective way.

Just as children become very frightened when they see their loved ones wearing a mask, so the inner child in adults becomes terrified when in their imagination they fail to 'unmask' reality and cannot separate the drama from the real.

Psychological Reflection

Let's imagine that a person suffers some unpleasant experiences and starts to always think badly of themselves, of others and of the world. It is as if they put on a pair of glasses with a black filter and see everything around them in a too dark colour. They might even think that this existence is hell and feel lost because they do not see the good that surrounds them with enough light and clarity.

What is going on with such a person? It happens that he or she does not see reality as it is because of the colour of their own filter.

Seneca proposes to unmask reality and gain objectivity. Life is not a tragedy; it is more a tragicomedy. There is also beauty, goodness and hope in life. If you don't see anything good, it doesn't mean it isn't there. Maybe you just need to change your glasses and look again.

12

IN WHOSE HANDS IS YOUR HAPPINESS?

Question/comment from a seeker:

Even though I try very hard, I can never get others to be satisfied with me, and I have a hard time with that.

Seneca's answer (letter 23):

Don't put your happiness in the hands of others.

Those who seek to feel good only with material things or things external to themselves will always remain unsatisfied. If you want to be happy, look within yourself.

Psychological Reflection

There are people who are not even satisfied with themselves. How can they be satisfied with you?

Also, sometimes we take things personally, forgetting that not everything has to do with us. If, for example, a co-worker doesn't want to collaborate with you on a task, they may simply be having a bad day and their attitude might have nothing to do with you or the way you work.

Putting your happiness in the hands of others is a good recipe for depression, as you will be dependent on many things that you have no control over.

Think back to the last time someone was angry with you and then you found out that they were angry with other people too or that their anger had nothing to do with you. How did you feel? What did you learn from that experience?

13

THIS TOO SHALL PASS

Question/comment from a seeker:

When I get depressed about something, I take a long time to recover. I'm not one of those people who take everything philosophically and look forward.

Seneca's answer (letter 78):

Your complaints only increase the severity and weight of your problems: the pain will always be less if you don't add to your worries. Rather encourage yourself by saying: 'It's nothing or it's almost nothing; hang in there, this too shall pass.' By believing that it is a minor issue, it becomes easier to handle.

Psychological Reflection

How can you become bitter about your life? You can complain about everything, feel pity for yourself, think about how bad you are, compare yourself to others a lot, or be very critical of yourself. You could probably come up with even more ideas.

When we live in a state of mind where negative thinking dominates most of the time, it is very easy to suffer and difficult to feel good.

Therefore, when we go through a difficult moment in life it is better to learn not to overthink so as not to fill our mind with unpleasant thoughts.

Seneca recommends that we take the 'drama' out of the situation, focus on the solution and feed our minds with kind thoughts in order to stay calm.

14

RECOGNISE YOUR WEAKNESS

Question/comment from a seeker:

I recognise that I am very nervous.

Seneca's answer (letter 6):

The first step to getting better is realising what is wrong with you. Some sufferers are congratulated when they come to terms with their illness. Now it is time to find a remedy.

Psychological Reflection

Many people find it difficult to recognise a weakness because they think: 'If I recognise my vulnerability it will be humiliating. I have to be strong and always look good in order to be loved.'

But hiding psychological problems often leads to a snowball effect, making them grow even bigger and worse by not recognising them in time.

Seneca reminds you that you have already taken the most important step when you recognise what is wrong with you. He says that those who are strong enough to accept their own vulnerability deserve to be congratulated. Only by acknowledging it can we move forward and evolve.

15

LIFE CHANGES

Question/comment from a seeker:

I don't like change at all. It worries me to think that the good things in my life might change one day.

Seneca's answer (letter 65):

Change is all around, when something is created and destroyed, in art and in every transformation in this life.

Psychological Reflection

Change is one of the few things we can be absolutely certain of in this life.

What is the point of suffering for fear of change, if it is going to happen anyway? It is more useful to try to focus on what benefits us from each change.

Besides, change is not always bad. As Maya Angelou says, we delight in the beauty of the butterfly, but rarely admit the changes it has gone through to achieve that beauty.

16

PLAY YOUR CARDS

Question/comment from a seeker:

Can faith (in God) help us face life more calmly and serenely?

Seneca's answer (letter 65):

Everything proceeds from God. God directs and permeates everything and all things dance to his tune. We can affirm that God is superior to everything else.

And just as God is in the world, so too is the soul within the human being. So let us be strong in the face of chance, because we know that the inferior (things, circumstances) is at the service of the superior, at the service of God, and let us not be disheartened by offences, chains, wounds or needs.

Psychological Reflection

Seneca reminds us that there is a higher order in Nature that is beyond our control. Faith in God is a resource to calm most fears and worries. One who has such faith sees everything that happens as the 'Divine will' and problems become challenges or tests that one must face with intelligence, courage and hope.

A psychological question that arises here is: does it make sense to suffer too much for what happens to us, if every situation that life presents to us depends on divine will or cosmic chance? Is it not more useful to think that life deals the cards and that we can only play them in the best possible way?

Believing that we can control everything is an illusion that generates a lot of anxiety and stress. We cannot control what happens to us, but we can always manage how we respond.

Think of a situation that is currently distressing you. Does it make sense for you to suffer from the cards that fate has dealt you, if you are determined to play them to the best of your ability?

17

THE FIRE OF LOVE

Question/comment from a seeker:

How can I fall out of love? I am suffering a lot in love.

Seneca's answer (letter 69):

If someone wants to fall out of love, they should avoid any memory of the loved one, because the fire of love can easily be fanned. In the same way, one who chooses to detach themselves from the things that kindle their desires must avoid exposing their eyes or ears to the things they want to leave behind.

Psychological Reflection

Seneca recommends 'non-exposure' to anything that reminds us of the person we wish to distance ourselves from. That means avoiding external exposure (talking to others about that person, looking at their photos, spending time on their social media, etc.) and also avoiding internal exposure (voluntarily remembering past times with that person, etc.). It is about not continuing to add fuel to the fire so that it dies out through inanition.

When we stop feeding the memory of a person or attachment we want to leave behind, it becomes easier to get over it and move on. It sounds simple, but most people do the opposite.

Do you remember an experience from your past where you successfully moved on from a frustrating relationship? Did you stop exposing yourself to that person and their memories? If not, how did you do it?

18

NATURE IS FAIR

Question/comment from a seeker:

Society is hard and living in it is becoming increasingly difficult.

Seneca's answer (letter 90):

Nature is not so unfair as to make life easy for animals and complicated for humans.

Nature does not require us to live with so much complexity and material adornments. We already have everything we need at our fingertips, but we are not satisfied with what is simple and so we unnecessarily complicate our lives.

Psychological Reflection

Many philosophers, mystics and psychologists agree that human beings tend to make life bitter for themselves, make difficult what is simple, and then find it hard to get out of the labyrinth they have got themselves into.

A better way of living is possible. We exist in a materialistic society where to be reasonably happy we need to learn to control at least two things: our mind and our economy. Often, too much thought is given to money and what can be achieved with it, but the control of the mind and the care of mental health is often neglected. Those who are at ease with themselves will be better able to simplify their lives and appreciate all the good things, wherever they are.

19

A FULL LIFE

Question/comment from a seeker:

How can I feel good in a life full of work and obligations that leave me no time for myself and the things I enjoy?

Seneca's answer (letters 61–62):

Life already provides us with everything we need, but we are always anxiously looking for more and more. We feel that something is missing and we will always feel that, because experiencing a full and satisfying life does not depend on the passing of years and days, but on the attitude of the soul.

Many people pretend to be too busy to devote themselves to philosophy, with many unnecessary tasks that they themselves continually add to their lives.

But I choose to devote time to my leisure wherever I am, to be always true to myself. I do not let things and occupations take over me, but participate in them occasionally. I don't look for excuses to waste time, but wherever I am, I pause and meditate on something healthy.

Psychological Reflection

Nowadays, we remain in a state of continuous mental saturation, where it is especially important to establish priorities and find a balance between duty and leisure in order not to wear ourselves out, burn out and embitter our lives.

Seneca tells us that life already offers us everything we need, but it is we who complicate our lives and set unnecessary goals that stress us out. It is as if we build mountains that we then have to climb, and that exhausts us.

How can you find a better balance between your obligations and your free time? Is there any goal or dream that causes you too much anxiety? If you gave it up, would it improve your quality of life?

20

FREEDOM

Question/comment from a seeker:

What is freedom? What can I do to feel freer?

Seneca's answer (letter 51):

You ask me what freedom is? Not being a slave to anything, to any need, and not depending on chance. Concentrate only on being a righteous person and consider that to be good fortune. The day I don't depend on chance, chance will lose its influence over me.

Psychological Reflection

One source of fear and anxiety is uncertainty. We do not accept it. We don't seem to be completely at ease without sufficient information about what will happen and how we can control it. And when we think that chance will bring us some misfortune, we might suffer and feel very helpless.

But if we have more inner peace, then it wouldn't matter so much if it rains or if the sun comes out because we will be reasonably well, whatever happens.

We will be more independent and freer from external changes if we manage our inner world with the help of a practical philosophy (meditation, prayer, psychological resources, etc.).

21

THE ONLY THING THAT MATTERS

Question/comment from a seeker:

I am not successful in life. I am not attractive or rich at all. In short, I am not a lucky person.

Seneca's answer (letter 76):

In assessing how good a ship is, we do not look at how beautiful its colours are or whether it is made of gold and silver. Nor do we analyse whether it is loaded with riches. But we do look at whether it is solid, stable, waterproof, resistant to the pounding and swell of the sea, whether it is manoeuvrable, fast and windproof.

In the same way, in the case of a human being, don't analyse how many people like someone, or how expensive the bed they sleep in is, or the value of the glasses they drink from. The only thing that matters is whether they are a good person. A person is a good person when they reason with maturity and values. That is our nature: human virtue.

Psychological Reflection

Seneca shares his criteria for evaluating people. As a good stoic, he focuses on the most important thing: whether someone is a good person. What is the point of looking at the shell of a nut, if what matters is only the nut?

For Seneca, a person is good to the extent that he or she lives by human values, is reasonable and is flexible enough to face what fate throws at them.

A person's value has nothing to do with money or material success, but with inner stability and the way he or she deals with problems.

And you, what criteria do you use to value yourself? Which part of you is the shell, the external and changeable, and which part is the fruit, the internal and stable?

22

ALWAYS EXPECT THE BEST

Question/comment from a seeker:

How can I deal with uncertainty without getting anxious?

Seneca's answer (letter 88):

Just as I know that everything could happen, I also know that not everything has to happen. So I hope for the best, but I am prepared for the worst.

Psychological Reflection

The person who acts in an optimistic way enjoys life better, identifies more opportunities and is motivated to continue living and creating. But this does not mean that one should be naïve; it is also smart to anticipate situations and be prepared. In order to stay calm, it is necessary to balance optimism and preparation.

In the famous fable of the ant and the grasshopper, the ant worked stoically through spring and summer (the grasshopper's time of enjoyment) and thus got its food and was prepared for the harsh winter. His companion, the grasshopper, who spent the whole summer singing and enjoying himself without preparing, suffered when winter came because he had no food stored.

23

WE'RE LIKE LIGHTBULBS

Question/comment from a seeker:

I am worried that after death I will suffer some discomfort. It makes me anxious not to know what will happen.

Seneca's answer (letter 54):

Death means ceasing to exist on this plane. But even after our existence ends, everything will be the same as before it.

If there were something unpleasant after death, you should have experienced that in the state you were in before you were born. But at that time, you did not experience any discomfort.

Is it not absurd to think that a lightbulb that is switched off is worse than it was before it was switched on? In the same way, we are switched on and off. And in the time in between (which is our life) we suffer a little, but it is impossible to experience discomfort before or after.

Psychological Reflection

According to Seneca, we should not worry about our discomfort after death, because it is in life that we suffer and where we can manage our inner selves.

The philosopher tells us: if you don't remember suffering any discomfort before you were born, then don't worry about suffering it after you die either.

According to some mystical philosophers, death is an experience where the light goes out in one place, only to shine again in another. Won't those who think only of discomfort rather than seeing a natural transformation suffer more?

When a person has some kind of positive faith or mental preparation, he or she tends to face death with more serenity.

24

DON'T FALL INTO BAD HABITS

Question/comment from a seeker:

What's wrong with pleasures? They help me cope better with everyday life.

Seneca's answer (letter 39):

Many people enjoy certain pleasures at the beginning. But then they get used to them until they no longer know how to live without them. In this state, you are sad and suffer because you start to believe that you need superficial things that were unnecessary for you before.

The breaking point of unhappiness comes when you live with your heart set on ridiculous, irrelevant and frivolous things.

If you fall into bad habits, it will be too late to put it right.

Psychological Reflection

Many pleasures are initially whims, but we get hooked on them. For example, the young person who tries smoking for the first time and then becomes a smoker. Or looking at your mobile phone out of boredom and then discovering that you look at it for eight hours a day.

Many of the human pleasures that do not respond to basic needs, such as eating and drinking, must be dosed with balance to prevent them from turning into addictions, anxiety and a feeling of inner emptiness.

When we keep ourselves busy with interesting and humanising activities, we can avoid pursuing pleasures that we don't really need in order to feel good.

25

DO NOT CONFUSE PRIORITIES

Question/comment from a seeker:

First, I have to take care of my family, my work and my goals. And when I retire and have more free time, I will be able to devote myself to subjects such as philosophy, the meaning of life, spirituality, etc. But now my priorities are different.

Seneca's answer (letter 17):

Don't be fooled by thoughts like 'I have to achieve that first, I'm not rich yet, or when I achieve that, then I will devote myself to philosophy and give depth to my life'. Don't confuse priorities.

Always dedicate yourself to what is most important regardless of your circumstances. A wise person knows how to adapt to any situation. Philosophy helps you to feel free and not fear anything or anyone.

Psychological Reflection

When you make a house, you don't start with the roof but with the foundation of the building. Put what is important in your existence first, and the rest will fall into place. By putting our values and priorities in order and practising systematic actions that lead to a soulful life, our anxiety is reduced.

There will never be a perfect time and you will never have time to spare. The time to live a good life is now, not tomorrow.

What actions can you take today to live more in alignment with the most meaningful areas of your life?

26

ACCEPT WITH SERENITY

Question/comment from a seeker:

Sometimes, in order to achieve something, I have to force things. It is a constant effort. Then I'm left wondering if it was all worth it.

Seneca's answer (letter 54):

The wise man does nothing unwillingly, but accepts with serenity what life offers to him.

Psychological Reflection

'Don't push the river because it flows by itself' is a popular quote that reminds us that there are situations where it is better to let things take their course.

Too often, we try to make reality fit our plans and desires, like a piece of a jigsaw puzzle that must fit perfectly. When we see that the pieces don't fit, we feel powerless, and that can lead to depression, anxiety and exhaustion.

To live with greater maturity, we need to accept that reality is not going to change for us. We are the ones who have to adapt and flow with life, making use of our capacities and appreciating the opportunities that come our way, in order to live with greater calm and serenity.

27

KNOWING HOW TO SAY 'NO'

Question/comment from a seeker:

Sometimes, I get carried away by others because I find it hard to say 'no' to them, but that gets me into trouble. What do you think about that?

Seneca's answer (letter 37):

Sometimes, we bring our own fate on ourselves by not making decisions and letting ourselves go. Then, in the midst of the storm, we ask ourselves in surprise: how did I get into this situation?

Psychological Reflection

People who always adapt to others are often friendly and non-confrontational, but they can also become insecure and dependent.

Seneca reminds us that it is important not to let ourselves be led blindly, but to reflect first. If others lead us astray and we allow them to do so, it is our responsibility.

If you are one of those people who find it difficult to say 'no', refusing someone's proposal may at first seem very harsh. But after a while, people will get used to it and appreciate you for having your own judgement, personality and self-confidence.

When was the last time you said 'no' to someone? How did you feel afterwards? Do you think you were true to yourself?

28

YOU NEVER LOSE IF YOU LEARN

Question/comment from a seeker:

I've invested a lot of time in something that didn't turn out well in the end. What advice would you give me so that I don't get frustrated?

Seneca's answer (letter 7):

Neither time nor effort is wasted if you have learnt something.

Psychological Reflection

For the problem of 'wasted time', Seneca broadens our view: if you learn something, you always win.

Would it be wasting time if that experience helps you to mature, to be humbler and to recognise that the world does not revolve around you? And if a situation or problem leads you to recover your faith in spite of everything that happens to you, would that be losing or winning? Is it wasting time to learn an existential lesson?

Life is infinitely greater than what we perceive when we feel bad. And the funny thing is that sometimes we are lucky enough to have things happen to us that we did not initially want, but which then lead us to a better destiny than we could ever have imagined.

29

THE DEPTH OF LIFE

Question/comment from a seeker:

I'm very busy, I don't have time to philosophise or anything like that.

Seneca's answer (letter 72):

You must always find time for philosophy. And you must postpone everything else in order to prioritise what is important in your life. He who devotes himself to something good will never spend too much time on it, even if the duration of the task extends from his childhood to the end of his life.

It is necessary to avoid spending too much time on superficial tasks.

Psychological Reflection

According to the Spanish psychotherapist Ramón Rosal, 'depth of life' consists of a humanising attitude. That is, living in an authentic and personal way that helps you to know yourself better.

Do you ask yourself some philosophical questions from time to time? Let's look at some examples from Rosal:

Which elements of my life depend on 'fate' and which depend on whether my decisions were right or wrong?

What is important to me and what is not important to me?

What is the main mission of the human being throughout his or her existence?

What are the experiences and aspirations that make me feel that my life is worth living?

Seneca invites us to review our 'depth of life' from time to time, so that we do not act like soulless robots, dragging ourselves through life.

30

DON'T BE A SLAVE TO YOUR BODY

Question/comment from a seeker:

I place a lot of importance on my body. I don't leave the house without dressing up, I watch my diet and I do a lot of sport, but I still don't find myself good-looking and that makes me feel very uncomfortable.

Seneca's answer (letter 14):

It is natural for us to take care of our bodies in order to be healthy. That is fine.

But we should not become slaves to our physique. If you give so much importance to the body, you will be obsessed with all things related to it and that will make you suffer. We should not live for the body, but keep in mind that it is only a part of us.

Psychological Reflection

If you identify so strongly with your body, how can you be at ease when one day you can no longer maintain that shape, appearance or functionality? Obsessing too much about your body is a recipe for anxiety, frustration and low self-esteem.

A mature attitude towards your body includes accepting that it will eventually age and change, and that this is normal and natural.

Seneca encourages us to maintain a healthy balance: to take care of our bodies, but not to become obsessed with them.

31

LIFE IS LIKE A PLAY

Question/comment from a seeker:

I am not making the most out of my life and I don't know how much time I have left, and that stresses me a lot.

Seneca's answer (letter 77):

Life is like a play. It's not so much about how long the play lasts, but about how well you perform the part you've been cast to play. And it doesn't matter when it's over. What counts is how well you perform that ending when the time comes.

Psychological Reflection

The philosopher does not seek quantity, but quality. He knows that one cannot choose everything in life (neither the years we live, nor the situations we will go through). But it is up to us to make the most of and appreciate the time we have been given in life.

It is in our hands to make the best of today and live a meaningful and soulful life in order to have a clear conscience at the end.

What can you do today to ensure a clear conscience when you go to sleep?

32

HOW TO MAKE THINGS EASIER

Question/comment from a seeker:

There are many things I can't stand. And it makes me mad when everything is not to my liking.

Seneca's answer (letter 91):

Imagine that Mother Nature speaks to you and says: 'The things you are complaining about are the same for everyone. I cannot make them easier for anyone. But, yes, everyone will make them as easy for themselves as they choose.'

How? with an inner serenity.

Psychological Reflection

A story that aligns with this idea expressed by Seneca is of the king who wanted to cover all the land with leather so as not to suffer from the stones on the road (at that time they went barefoot). But the solution offered by the wisest man in the kingdom was that it would be better for the king to cover his own feet with leather (he invented shoes) so that he would always be comfortable.

In psychology, it is often said that what is important for mental well-being is not so much what happens to us, but how we interpret and respond to it. We can learn to take things easier, be patient and optimistic. And if we improve our 'inner garden', everything will become more bearable.

Which habit or activity can you start today that will help you gain inner serenity and make things easier and more bearable?

33

MATERIAL THINGS

Question/comment from a seeker:

How can I give less importance to material things so that they don't affect me so much?

Seneca's answer (letter 74):

When things come to you, don't let them hook you emotionally. That way, if at some point life takes them from you, you will not be torn apart.

Use things without letting them affect your ego, as if they were loans that you have to take care of for a certain period of time and that, at some point, you will have to let go of.

Psychological Reflection

Erich Fromm says: 'If I am what I have, who am I when I lose what I have?'

Seneca advises us to limit ourselves to the usefulness and necessity of things, over our vanity and presumption. To not to take what we have today for granted, but use it as if it would soon cease to belong to us.

By giving less importance to possessions, we will be less 'possessed' by them and we will enjoy more inner freedom and calmness.

34

WHAT YOU REALLY NEED

Question/comment from a seeker:

I am afraid of ending up poor.

Seneca's answer (letter 25):

All the wealth we need is within our reach. What we really require is free or very affordable: our nature wants for only bread and water. Whoever manages to adapt their desires to what they need to survive will be able to compete in happiness even with Jupiter.

Psychological Reflection

If you are healthy, have food, shelter from the cold and a roof to sleep under, you can feel lucky and at peace. For Seneca and many philosophers, the rest are frills and whims.

Examples like Buddha, Diogenes or St Francis of Assisi show that an austere and simple existence can also be great, profound and dignified.

According to most sages of every culture and age, a good life depends more on the richness of our inner world than on our bank balance.

35

COMPARISON WITH OTHERS

Question/comment from a seeker:

When I see people who have achieved great things in life, I feel like a failure.

Seneca's answer (letter 15):

Don't compare yourself with those who have more than you or those who are better than you at something. Compare yourself with those who are worse off than you, so that you will be more grateful to God and to life.

And in the end, what do you gain by comparing yourself with others? It is better to compare yourself with your own evolution.

Psychological Reflection

Comparison is a frequent cause of anxiety, depression and toxic self-demands.

You don't know what price those people you think have achieved wonderful things have actually paid. They may have suffered a lot, they may have had to deal with loss and maybe you would not be willing to go through the same.

So, to feel good, don't compare yourself to others. Or if you can't help it, remember those who are worse off than you, like the person who cried because he had no shoes until he saw one who had no feet.

The philosopher's solution: if you want to feel good, realise how lucky you are and be grateful for it. Remember the gifts that life has already given you, no matter how small. Remember your achievements, your progress and the moments when life smiled at you.

36

USE YOUR IMAGINATION WELL

Question/comment from a seeker:

What if all goes wrong, what if I lose my job and don't get another one as good, what if nobody loves me and I die alone, what if . . . ?

Seneca's answer (letter 13):

Most of the time we are afraid of things we imagine, but which will never actually happen. How could you make better use of your imagination?

Psychological Reflection

The 'what if' thought is a terrible monster that frightens and threatens millions of people every day. In psychotherapy, exercises are done to help replace the repetitive 'what if' thoughts with more useful and relaxing ones.

Seneca proposes that you use your mind better: if you have a strong imagination, which you have already shown by using it to worry, why not use it better to cheer yourself up?

37

YOUR EXPECTATIONS

Question/comment from a seeker:

I expected to have achieved more at my age. Do I demand too much of myself?

Seneca's answer (letter 5):

We are afraid of not getting what we expect. Adjust your expectations, and you will live better.

Psychological Reflection

The mind is never satisfied, always stressed by its desires. When you have a bike, you want a motorbike and then a car. Then you want a boat, then a private plane, then a whole airline . . .

Do you think it's impossible to be happy if you don't achieve your dreams? Do you think life would be unbearable if what you hoped for doesn't happen?

According to Seneca, by being less demanding and more humble, you will have fewer problems and be calmer.

38

DON'T LET THEM TRAMPLE ON YOU

Question/comment from a seeker:

I try to be kind to others, but I feel that I am then taken advantage of. How can I cope better?

Seneca's answer (letter 14):

Wisdom teaches us to seek balance: don't trample on others and don't let them trample on you. Take it philosophically.

Psychological Reflection

It is impossible for people to always be kind to us. We cannot control how others treat us, but we can manage how we respond to them.

Seneca advises us not to allow others to disrespect us or trample on our dignity. A healthy relationship is based on mutual respect, which depends on both parties.

If someone does not respect you and you can avoid that relationship, why are you still hooked on it? And if you can't avoid it or there is no remedy, focus more on how you act and don't take the other person and their lack of politeness too seriously.

39

GET YOUR HEAD STRAIGHT

Question/comment from a seeker:

I can't find a partner. I have had several short relationships. At the beginning, everything goes well, but after a short time I get bored and I start to notice everything I don't like about my partner. It scares me to think that in the end I might end up alone.

Seneca's answer (letter 20):

People do not know what they want. Our judgement and our priorities change from one day to the next, and sometimes we want the opposite of what we originally wanted at the beginning. Get your head straight first, understand what you are looking for and don't change your mind or your course any more.

Psychological Reflection

How can you make a good choice in love? What is the most important thing in a partner? Many people don't know what to look for when choosing a partner and then think they are unlucky.

Seneca says that in order to make a good choice, we must first identify and understand what we are looking for. Continuing with the example of a partner, we could ask ourselves: Is he or she a good person? Do I consider him or her a good friend? Do I love him or her? Is it wise to make a long-term commitment to someone like him or her? Does he or she care about my well-being?

When we already know what we want, it will be easier to search and hit the target. And if we make a wrong choice, we will surely have learnt something to help make a better choice in the future.

We can apply this piece of advice from the philosopher to most of the decisions that trouble us.

40

GOOD INFLUENCES

Question/comment from a seeker:

How do I know who is a good teacher, someone to look up to, a good influence on me?

Seneca's answer (letter 41):

When you observe a person unperturbed by danger, unmoved by baser instincts, facing adversity well, calm in the storm, an elevated soul, will you not find that admirable?

One so elevated could not be so without a developed spirituality. Just as the rays of the sun touch the earth, but belong to its source, so the high soul is among us to bring us closer to the Divine.

Though this soul talks with us, it never forgets its origin: it is attentive to Him, it continually directs its gaze to Him, that is its tendency, and thus it intervenes in our life as a being shining with its own light.

Psychological Reflection

Seneca speaks of the transcendental capability, the spiritual capacity of the human being as a source of wisdom and inner calm. He reminds us that some people in the world are exceptional when it comes to the development of their consciousness and can teach us by example how to live better. These are people whose purpose in life is more linked to spirituality than to the worldly and the material.

41

ENDURING ADVERSITY

Question/comment from a seeker:

I am afraid of getting sick and suffering. What can I do to cope better if it happens to me?

Seneca's answer (letter 67):

I am not so foolish as to want to be ill, but if it is inevitable that I will be, then my aspiration will be to not show weakness of spirit. I do not desire adversity, but I desire the virtue to endure it.

Psychological Reflection

The stoic approach: instead of feeling pity for ourselves, blaming bad luck and becoming emotionally dependent on pain, we take control of the situation and decide, as far as possible, to maintain an attitude of calm, strength and dignity.

Carl Gustav Jung says that what you resist persists. What you deny subdues you and what you accept transforms you.

How can Seneca's and Jung's advice help you with your fear of pain?

What does it mean for you to respond calmly and courageously to a situation that worries you?

42

MAKING LIFE PLANS

Question/comment from a seeker:

I have many plans and projects for my life, but I have a hard time when something doesn't go as I had planned.

Seneca's answer (letter 101):

How crazy to plan for a long life if you don't even know what will happen tomorrow!

Trust me when I tell you that we live in uncertainty, even those people who seem to be luckier. No one can be sure of anything about their future, for what we think we possess today slips through our fingers. Even this very hour that we think we have secured also depends on chance.

Psychological Reflection

We depend much more on chance than we realise. We live in an illusion of control that makes us feel secure, but it is still an illusion. Everything around you can change and your plans may never come true. The more we are aware of this truth, the easier it will be to cope with changes and failures in life.

Although Seneca says that we do not know what will happen tomorrow, planning is not always bad. On the contrary, it is sometimes smart and necessary. But if we keep a flexible attitude, knowing that not everything is in our hands, we will be more prepared for the unexpected and be more at ease.

When was the last time something didn't go according to plan? What did you learn from that experience?

43

NOTHING BUT A TRANSFORMATION

Question/comment from a seeker:

I am terrified of death.

Seneca's answer (letters 26-36-69):

We only die on the day we are due to die.

The philosopher meditates on death in order to gain more freedom. He reflects on death in order not to have the soul of a slave to the world, but that of someone free, able to see beyond the power of the material and of time.

The love towards life is not to be rejected, but we must be realistic and prepared when our time comes.

Moreover, death is transformation. In this world, nothing is extinguished, but continually comes and goes. Summer leaves and returns after spring, the sun leaves and returns after night, the planets leave and return at the completion of their transits.

Psychological Reflection

Seneca reassures us with the idea that death is inevitable, implying that destiny has already fixed the date of our last day. We find ourselves on an existential plane where every day some come and others go, as if the world were an airport where it is a law of life that some constantly land and others take off.

Through introspective practices such as meditation and prayer, people learn to detach from their bodies and bring their attention more to their inner world, as well as develop their faith.

These practices help to prepare for the final day when Nature itself separates one permanently from the body.

44

RECHARGE BATTERIES

Question/comment from a seeker:

I am so exhausted that even sleeping doesn't help me to recharge my energy and feel good anymore.

Seneca's answer (letter 56):

During the night we do not always rest, for the dreams of those who sleep are as stressful as their lives. True serenity is the serenity that comes when we achieve a clear conscience.

Psychological Reflection

Every person is faced with different battles or karmas that he or she has to deal with on a daily basis. Therefore, it is very important to know how we can recharge our energy, our inner battery.

Depending on our personality, there will be some activities that help us more than others. This is something very personal that we must reflect on and discover.

Sleep does not always guarantee rest, but inner peace does. Because of this, many people seek help from meditation and other introspective exercises to calm their inner self.

How do you recharge your energy and what helps you the most?

45

LET'S WAKE UP FROM OUR SLEEP

Question/comment from a seeker:

I don't want to analyse my faults and weaknesses because I don't want to damage what little self-esteem I have.

Seneca's answer (letter 53):

Why does no one recognise their shortcomings? Because they are still a prisoner of them. Just as talking about one's dreams means that one is already awake, recognising one's faults is the awakening and the health of the soul's consciousness.

Let us remain awake and aware so that we can recognise our shortcomings. But nothing will awaken us like true philosophy—it alone will dispel our deep slumber. Dedicate yourself to it and trust it. You can do it; it is made for you.

Psychological Reflection

Self-knowledge is a form of 'psychological awakening'. It takes maturity and courage to recognise one's own strengths and weaknesses. Identifying our shortcomings helps us to work on them, become stronger and humbler.

For example, if you are a very emotional, sensitive and intuitive person, it may be more difficult for you to make logical decisions. And if you are a reflective and calm person, you may find it difficult to stay in a job that demands speed, passion and a continuous state of alertness. Each personality style has strengths and areas for improvement.

Self-awareness can alleviate anxiety. When you understand yourself better, you can improve your relationships, make better decisions, adapt better to reality and create a lifestyle that benefits you.

46

AMBITION

Question/comment from a seeker:

I am ambitious and never feel satisfied, I always crave for more. What do you think about this?

Seneca's answer (letters 72–73)

Attalus used an example: 'Have you ever seen how a dog catches with its jaws the piece of bread or meat thrown to it by its owner? Everything he catches, he gobbles up quickly and then waits anxiously for the next piece. The same thing happens to us—everything that chance throws at us we gobble up impatiently, without tasting it, and we remain anxiously waiting for the next thing to come along.'

The same does not happen to the wise man: he is always satisfied. If he receives something he welcomes it quietly and keeps it; he enjoys the inner joy that is lasting, superior and inexhaustible.

Anyone who desires to receive something forgets to appreciate what he already possesses. And ambition is never exhausted and is ungrateful because all desires are the same; as soon as one is fulfilled, the next one is generated.

Psychological Reflection

It is difficult to satisfy the whims of our mind.

From a stoic point of view, ambition can blind us. It makes us take what we have for granted and pushes us to run after something, at the cost of our time, energy and sometimes even our health and personal relationships.

The remedy, according to Seneca, is to appreciate what we have and enjoy it. Contentment is an inner state that does not depend so much on external achievements.

When was the last time you were ambitious and achieved something? How long did your satisfaction last? What did you do afterwards?

47

WHERE YOU FIND SERENITY

Question/comment from a seeker:

I only get a little bit of rest and am in a good mood when I go on holiday.

Seneca's answer (letter 55):

Even in the liveliest and most cheerful places, I have met sad people; and I have also seen people who, despite their loneliness, knew how to entertain themselves.

Serenity does not depend on where you are. No matter where you find yourself, why not go with your imagination and thoughts to a quiet and lofty place?

Psychological Reflection

You can relax wherever you are if you can calm your inner self. Use your imagination to learn to gain serenity.

Here is an example of a short visualisation that you could practise when you need it:

Imagine that you are on an ideal beach, perhaps one that you have known and enjoyed in your past. Feel the warmth of the sun on your skin. Listen to the sound of the ocean, of the waves coming and going. Notice how your body sinks into the sand. Notice how you feel and how you breathe. With each breath you feel more relaxed, more disconnected from the world and more energetic (develop everything you can think of to feel good on the beach, to breathe calmly).

Holidays are not always a guarantee of well-being. Some people need a holiday from their holidays. During this leisure time, some people have fights with their loved ones, others schedule a full agenda of activities with little rest, etc.

Use your imagination to relax a little every day and you will have a 'paid (indoor) holiday' for life.

48

LOSS

Question/comment from a seeker:

I am very afraid of losing my job, my possessions or my loved ones.

Seneca's answer (letter 4):

It is part of nature to lose everything we have sooner or later. You will be able to enjoy and appreciate your surroundings better when you accept this and realise that nothing lasts forever. Even the richest and most powerful can lose everything.

Psychological Reflection

Accepting the limits of life is accepting reality, and it helps us to appreciate and be more grateful for what we have in the present. Appreciation and gratitude are important for our well-being. And if one day you lose something, it will be easier to have a clear conscience because you will know that you appreciated it while you had it.

49

THE PASSAGE OF TIME

Question/comment from a seeker:

I worry that I am getting older without having lived a good life.

Seneca's answer (letter 74):

Values or principles do not depend on the passage of time. An honest life of a hundred years is as good as an honest life of one single day.

Psychological Reflection

Seneca dismisses the importance of the number of years you live. If it is an honest life, if you are a good person even for a single day, then you have made good use of your time. Quality is more important than quantity. It is never too late to make amends for past mistakes and to have a clear conscience.

What is a good life for you? Can you think of one thing you could change today to get closer to the life you want to have?

50

LIVING BY IMITATING OTHERS

Question/comment from a seeker:

I can't help comparing myself to others, especially when I look at other people's social networks. I envy them for what they have managed to have in their lives.

Seneca's answer (letter 123):

We realise that many things are unnecessary when we no longer have them. We did not enjoy them because we needed them, but for the simple fact of having them. And how many things we have acquired just because others—most of them—had them too! One of our mistakes is that we live by imitation. Instead of being guided by what is reasonable, we are guided by fashion.

Psychological Reflection

An Anglo-Saxon saying goes: 'The grass is always greener on the other side.' It will always seem to us that others have something better: a better life, a more expensive car, a bigger garden or a slimmer body. This is an example of misused selective perception. Instead of focusing on what we have, we focus on what we lack.

And yet, in Western culture, we live with an abundance of material things of all kinds, accumulating more and more objects that we then throw away or sell in order to buy the next thing.

But if your house burned down, what would you really miss? Would you remember that tablecloth you bought for half the price or the bright green salad strainer you thought was so cute in the shop? Probably not.

The material things we need to live are few, and doing without unnecessary items to create more order and space in your home can add to your mental well-being.

If you want to compare yourself less and be in a good mood, it's best to stop following other people's lives on social media and focus on your own.

51

DIFFICULT PEOPLE

Question/comment from a seeker:

Today I had to deal with a rude person and it made me upset.

Seneca's answer (letter 81):

You complain about meeting an ungrateful or unpleasant person. Well, you must be a very lucky person if this is the first time such a thing has happened to you.

Psychological Reflection

Accepting reality also means knowing that during our lives we will occasionally meet unpleasant people. Seneca often recommends that we don't dramatise it too much, that we don't think it's terrible. It is not a drama, but something normal.

Your well-being does not depend on others. To gain serenity, accept and manage what life offers you, and try to avoid drama, complaints and obsessions.

52

REST

Question/comment from a seeker:

I am too busy. I never have time to rest.

Seneca's answer (letter 3):

Is day more important to nature than night?

Action is as necessary as rest. Without balance, how can you expect to feel good?

Psychological Reflection

Rest is a natural, free and very healthy anxiolytic. When we give ourselves permission to disconnect, relax, do nothing, meditate, take a walk, and so forth, it has as much value as being busy.

Can you say that you respect yourself and feel self-love if you don't allow yourself to balance things with rest?

If we don't learn to relax from time to time, our health will suffer the consequences.

Seneca gives us permission to rest and reminds us that it is necessary to live a balanced life.

53

THE ALL-OBSERVING EYE

Question/comment from a seeker:

Sometimes I harm others, but they hardly ever notice and I think 'out of sight, out of mind'. But then I get angry with myself for having done it.

Seneca's answer (letter 83):

We should live as if we are always being watched. We should even think as if someone can see inside us because, in reality, there is someone who can.

What is the point of hiding things from others? God sees everything; he is present in our soul and in our thoughts.

Psychological Reflection

We need to take care of our thoughts, words and actions so that they do not embarrass us before any observers. The benefits of that are a clear conscience, calmness and self-respect.

Do you act differently when you think no one sees you? How does that make you feel?

54

LIVING A SOULFUL LIFE

Question/comment from a seeker:

I am worried about the passage of time. How can I make the most of life?

Seneca's answer (letter 93):

We should not be concerned with living for a long time, but with the quality of the time lived, since living a long life depends on fate. But the quality of the time lived depends on choosing to live a soulful life.

Psychological Reflection

'What do I gain if I win the whole world but lose my own soul?' the Bible says. Following on from that idea, what good is a long life if we live without heart, kindness, calmness or soul?

What actions and decisions can you take to ensure that you live a soulful life?

55

FOCUS ON WHAT IS USEFUL

Question/comment from a seeker:

When I have a problem, so many things come to my mind that I don't know what to do.

Seneca's answer (letter 58):

I usually do this: for each thought, I try to find out how it can be useful to me.

Psychological Reflection

When we are saturated with worries and unpleasant thoughts, we can ask ourselves: is this thought that I have useful to me, or should I change it for another one? Am I thinking in a way that gives me strength and encouragement?

We must learn to identify our way of thinking and see if it is good for our well-being.

Seneca advises us to be practical: try to focus on the usefulness of thought.

56

INEXHAUSTIBLE JOY

Question/comment from a seeker:

Stoics talk about accepting fate, taking things philosophically, but I just want to be okay and not get stressed. And I think you can also achieve that when you have a good time, enjoy life and indulge yourself from time to time . . .

Seneca's answer (letter 59):

In the soul of the wise, there is always serenity and inexhaustible joy. This is a good reason to seek wisdom.

This joy is born from the awareness of one's own virtues: only those who are courageous, just and fair-minded can enjoy it.

But you may ask yourself: don't wicked and ignorant people enjoy themselves too? Well, not much more than lions enjoy a hunted prey.

Psychological Reflection

Sometimes, we get nervous and look for a quick and pleasant solution to a problem, even if this leads to greater discomfort. Faced with a problem, Seneca encourages us to analyse the situation well, be patient and act as a good human being would. In time, we will make wiser decisions and be more cheerful, without the need to resort to pleasurable 'patches'.

In an experiment on the postponement of immediate pleasure, children were given a treat and told that if they could go a certain time without eating it, they would be given another treat. Some children didn't hold out and ate the sweets straight away. Others managed to accumulate a lot of sweets—they knew that patience has a reward.

And you, how do you manage the 'treats' that life offers you?

57

LIFE IS NOT A CALCULATION

Question/comment from a seeker:

I am competitive, ambitious and I attach great importance to having a good education.

Seneca's answer (letter 88):

What's the point of knowing how to value a plot of land if I don't know how to share it with my brother? What's the point of being able to accurately calculate the price per square meter of my house if I then get annoyed with my neighbour?

On the one hand, I learn how to calculate and measure everything so that I don't lose any of what is mine. But I also want to learn how to lose everything with a smile on my face.

Psychological Reflection

Seneca tells us that life is not just about calculation, analysis and measurement.

Remember the importance of your inner well-being. What is the point of becoming an expert in a subject, if you do not know how to manage basic emotions and how to act with kindness and values in your everyday life?

In our higher education there is often not enough time dedicated to emotional management, human values training, practical psychology or philosophical counselling. Having a degree is fine and may prepare you for a particular job, but it will not teach you how to make decisions when you have anxiety, depression or face life's moral dilemmas.

58

YOU WILL NOT ESCAPE FROM YOURSELF

Question/comment from a seeker:

Sometimes, when I feel anxious, I travel somewhere, go out partying or meet friends and try to forget about everything for a while. But I see that this doesn't help me much. Why?

Seneca's answer (letter 28):

Socrates answered a similar question with these words: 'Why are you surprised that it does not feel good to travel if you go everywhere by yourself? You are distressed by the same motive that encouraged you to travel.'

Why doesn't that journey comfort you? Because you made the trip with yourself. The soul needs to let go of its burden. If your heart is not at ease, no place will be pleasant for you.

Psychological Reflection

If your heart is bad, you will be bad wherever you go, according to Seneca and Socrates.

Trying to disconnect is very healthy, but trying to run away from problems means postponing them and, sometimes, even increasing them.

There are many people who, faced with an unresolved break-up, for example, try to quickly meet other people or go on a trip, but they do not manage to feel better. Distraction is a temporary patch that does not solve the problems.

Know yourself, be patient and kind to yourself. Learn to cope with crises, relax and you will be fine anywhere.

59

THE BEST COMPANION

Question/comment from a seeker:

I can't stand being alone. I start to think too much about my life and become tense, and I prefer to distract myself or be with other people.

Seneca's answer (letter 58):

It is a pleasure to stay with oneself for as long as possible, if we have first managed to be pleasant company for ourselves.

Psychological Reflection

There is a concept called 'psychological entropy', which indicates that when the mind is unoccupied, it has a tendency towards chaos and internal disorder. This state often leads to anxiety.

It may have happened to you that when you were alone and doing nothing, you started to have repetitive negative thoughts. This is because you don't have an 'inner order' or don't know what to do.

That is why it is so important to know what activities can help you to occupy your time and attention in a creative, interesting and beneficial manner. In that way, you become your own best company.

What can you do the next time you find yourself alone and thinking unpleasant thoughts? Take some time, and make a list of activities that do not depend on other people, so that you can remember them and put them into practice.

60

YOU WON'T BE LOST WITH A GUIDE

Question/comment from a seeker:

I feel very lost in life, what can I do?

Seneca's answer (letter 11):

Epicurus says: 'Imagine that at all times you have a good person before you, someone who inspires you and who observes your behaviour, your thoughts and your words. Even when you are alone.'

You will never lack a good guide if you keep him in mind.

Psychological Reflection

Can you imagine going everywhere accompanied by a wise person?

How would that change and improve your behaviour? Would you feel lost in their presence? What would be different?

When you don't know what to do, you can think of an ideal role model, someone you admire, who usually makes good decisions and seems to have a good mentality. What would that person do? How would he or she decide? How would he or she behave in your situation?

It is very difficult to feel lost with a good guide.

61

TAKE THE REINS

Question/comment from a seeker:

I go overboard with online shopping. Then, I get anxious when I see how much I've spent. But nowadays it's so easy to get carried away and I find it unavoidable.

Seneca's answer (letter 50):

No one recognises their faults, such as being stingy or lustful. At least the blind look for a guide. But we go down the dead-end street while we repeat to ourselves: 'It is not that I am ambitious, but that in this city one cannot live any other way. It is not that I am wasteful, but that life in the city demands great expense. It's not my fault if I can't control my anger, it's normal for a young person to behave like that.'

Why do we deceive ourselves? The disease is not outside ourselves. But if we do not recognise it, we cannot be cured of it.

Psychological Reflection

There are things that depend on us and things that do not. Life takes many twists and turns, and sometimes we find ourselves in circumstances that we did not choose.

But that doesn't mean that we can 'wash our hands of it', thinking that it is the responsibility of others or a part of life. Losing your job may not be up to you, but it is on you what you do next. Living in an age where you can spend your monthly salary at the click of a button is not up to you. But it's your choice whether you fall into these traps or whether you manage your money in a smarter way. The reins are in your hands.

62

PRIORITISE WELL

Question/comment from a seeker:

I don't have time for reading, relaxation exercises or spirituality. Some people have time for that, but my situation is different.

Seneca's answer (letter 53):

If you were ill, you would postpone everything in order to recover your health. Don't you think it would be good to do the same and take care of your soul's health in the present?

Put aside everything that prevents you from doing so, and devote yourself now to developing your inner self. People who are too busy with other tasks will not succeed.

Psychological Reflection

Mental health, personal development and taking care of our inner world are undervalued.

Many people prefer to spend their time and energy on material matters. Only when they hit rock bottom and find themselves in an extreme situation are they encouraged to see a mental health professional.

Following the metaphor of illness, starting late to take care of your mental health would be like a smoker considering quitting smoking only when his or her lungs could no longer breathe. The smoker would have ignored the cough and all the other symptoms and advice from their environment that told them to take care of his or her health, and seeks a remedy only when the problem is practically irreparable.

Therefore, the free time we have is relative and depends on us—on our priorities.

Seneca advises us to prioritise well. The development of the spirit is no small thing and requires time. Everything else will sort itself out. To achieve a good life, we must first take care of our inner self.

What actions can you take today before going to sleep to take care of your inner self?

63

LIVING WITHOUT PURPOSE

Question/comment from a seeker:

Is it necessary to have a purpose in life, or is it better to go with the flow and see where life takes us?

Seneca's answer (letter 95):

To live without purpose means to live depending on chance. And if we choose a purpose, it had better contain human values.

You will agree with me that there is nothing so absurd as an indecisive and hesitant person who is afraid, either of their past or of what is left to live. And this will happen to us continually if we do not first free ourselves from all that imprisons and holds our soul back, preventing it from moving forward with its purpose.

Psychological Reflection

Designing our life project or defining our purpose helps us understand what we want to do with our life, what we would like to achieve and what kind of person we want to become.

This will serve as a compass to navigate through the randomness of life with direction and clarity.

What could you include in your life project? What dreams or goals would you like to achieve? What kind of person do you want to become?

64

THE SOUL AND DEATH

Question/comment from a seeker:

Is there a part of us that will survive death?

Seneca's answer (letter 57):

Just as when an attempt is made to crush a flame with something, it slips and escapes around the object that oppresses it, so does the subtlety of the soul. The soul cannot be imprisoned or held within the body, but it also escapes from that which oppresses it. Just as lightning thunders and illuminates vast spaces and then returns to its source through a tiny point, so the soul, which is subtler than fire, also withdraws from all bodies.

The immortality of the soul must be investigated. But if the soul survives the body, then it means that it cannot be affected by anything. In that case, it is surely immortal, eternal and cannot be physically harmed.

Psychological Reflection

Explanations on the immortality of the soul by philosophers such as Seneca, Marcus Aurelius or Socrates can be therapeutic, bringing serenity in the face of one's own death or that of loved ones and when existential questions arise.

Regardless of religion, spirituality or creed, having a unifying philosophy that gives meaning to life and death is always helpful when facing existential anxiety and depression.

There are still many mysteries in life and death that current science is unable to explain. Do you have a psychological, philosophical or spiritual explanation that helps you to calm your fear of death? Have you sought an explanation to help you feel better about this subject?

65

OTHERS DON'T DECIDE FOR YOU

Question/comment from a seeker:

I let myself be influenced too much by others and that makes me very insecure.

Seneca's answer (letter 56):

If we are conscious, and if we no longer attach importance to the superficial, nothing will distract us from ourselves. Others will no longer disturb our convictions when they are mature and firm.

Whoever has a weak and impressionable mind, because he does not know how to withdraw into the inner self, will be disturbed and distracted by the opinions of people and by strokes of chance in his life.

Psychological Reflection

If you want to take a decision and the opinions of others make you doubt and worry, you can ask yourself: is this decision aligned with my values? Is it a smart decision in the medium and long term? Your affirmative answer to these questions is a first step in the right direction.

It is said that dogs smell fear and insecurity. With people it is similar: the more insecurity you show, the more they will want to tell you what to do.

Listen to the opinions of your loved ones and people you trust, but don't let them decide for you. It's your life and you will have to live with the consequences of what you do.

Have you ever been overly influenced by others and regretted it? What did you learn from it? How can you stand firm in your convictions?

66

GRATITUDE

Question/comment from a seeker:

I think many of my problems would be solved if I were rich. Money makes life easier.

Seneca's answer (letter 1):

When you appreciate and are content with what you have now, you will never again feel that you have too little.

Psychological Reflection

It is an error to convince ourselves that when we have more money, we will appreciate life more, and have more peace of mind. Have we never seen people with a high standard of living who suffer from depression and anxiety and live in constant fear of losing their luxurious possessions?

The Stoics advise us to practise gratitude and not to make demands on ourselves that disturb our peace of mind. A mind focused on what we have and not on what we lack will be a good companion for life.

Have you ever written a gratitude journal? Every day, before going to sleep, write what went well or what good things you have in your life. You will see that you are also a lucky person.

Practising an appreciative attitude is relaxing. It is free and can make you feel 'rich'.

67

OLD AGE

Question/comment from a seeker:

I am afraid of old age. There will be many things I won't be able to do anymore.

Seneca's answer (letter 26):

Only bad habits and the senses that indulge them will grow old with time: the soul remains strong, knowing that it is not dependent on the body and is free of that burden.

My soul is happy and does not believe in old age. It claims to be in the prime of her life, even in old age. Let us have faith in it; that will be for the best.

But the moment you notice the limitations of your body, the best thing to do is to stop wishing for what you can no longer do.

Psychological Reflection

Every age has its own merits and limitations. Seneca suggests that we accept the reality of old age, that whatever we can no longer do, we consider unnecessary or undesirable and focus on what we can do and what continues to work: our inner self.

Psychologists and psychiatrists came to the same conclusion when they worked with the war wounded. They found that, after recovering from their wounds, those who focused too much on what they could no longer do became depressed and their mental health worsened dramatically, while those who focused more on what they could still do improved their mood and health.

68

BE TRUE TO YOURSELF

Question/comment from a seeker:

How do I know if I am making progress in my life?

Seneca's answer (letters 35–45):

Above all, try to be true to yourself. One way to see if you have made progress is to be on the right track.

See if what was important to you yesterday is still important to you today. In this way, you will identify if you are a hesitant spirit that changes with the wind. The wise person knows how to stand firm on what is important in life.

Decide the objective you want to achieve and follow the path that leads to it. Do not hesitate or change from one path to another because to do so is to get nowhere.

Psychological Reflection

Once again, Seneca points out that we should not move through life as the wind blows, but that we should be very clear about our priorities and the direction we are choosing.

But this should not be a source of anxiety. It is normal not to be always clear about everything. The Stoics simply advise us to avoid wandering aimlessly. The goal is not so much to reach a final destination, but as to go in the right direction (a life rich in human values). And that can already be seen as progress in life.

69

THE HUMAN BEING'S ONLY FREEDOM

Question/comment from a seeker:

My boss exploits me, and that makes me very uncomfortable. How can I deal with it better?

Seneca's answer (letter 37):

There are people who enjoy taking advantage of others. But sooner or later, wisdom—the only true freedom in human beings—will cast them aside. This wisdom can only be reached by being reasonable.

Even if others are not, you must not stop being rational. If you are reasonable with yourself, you will be all right with most people.

Psychological Reflection

Imagine you have a bulletproof vest, where the bullets are the criticism and bad treatment from another person, for example your boss. The vest would protect you from all 'bullets' and you would feel good and safe. Every morning you would wear your bulletproof vest at work, as naturally as you would wear a work uniform.

Well, Seneca says this bulletproof vest exists and must be created by yourself. It all depends on the right attitude, on taking care of your well-being, on avoiding being irrational, on being kind to yourself. The stronger and freer you are on the inside, the less you will be affected by the outside.

To create a good 'bulletproof vest' and face your day-to-day life as best you can, turn to philosophy, spirituality and psychology. Hopefully, one day your situation will change. But as long as you can't avoid dealing with the unpleasant, you can at least maintain your inner well-being.

70

THE BALANCE OF HAPPINESS

Question/comment from a seeker:

How do you find happiness?

Seneca's answer (letter 74):

Happiness is within you and lies in the soul, which is immutable and serene. But it can only be attained through a balance between the mundane and the spiritual.

Psychological Reflection

It is said that good gurus and teachers share few and simple advice and repeat the same recommendations over and over again. They do not saturate their pupils with information and do not change their minds.

Seneca, as a good Stoic mentor of Lucilius, repeats once again that we seek outside what is really inside. Happiness is in our hands, for it is within us.

And only when we take care of both parts (outside and inside), we obtain a healthy balance. This balance is like the foundation of a building. The most important thing is that the foundation is good, that it is a solid and resistant structure. Next will be to keep on building more and more floors.

71

WHAT ARE YOU DOING IT FOR?

Question/comment from a seeker:

What about people who help someone just to get something in return? I don't know who is a good person and who is a self-interested person.

Seneca's answer (letter 95):

If someone helps a sick person, I appreciate them. But if he does it to inherit his wealth, then he is a vulture waiting to devour the carcass. The same situations can be despicable or in good faith. It all depends on the intention or the way they are done.

Psychological Reflection

Seneca reminds us that it is not only what we do that matters, but also what we do it for. Helping someone out of kindness is not the same as expecting a reward.

In Stoic philosophy, virtue makes the difference. Marcus Aurelius, for example, says that if something is not in accordance with your values, don't do it. You yourself must analyse the situation and decide what is right.

The one who will be affected by the consequences of your decisions is you. You are the one who must take care to have a clear conscience.

When you do something, ask yourself: why am I doing it? Is it good for me and for others? Would an admirable person do it?

72

TAKE YOUR MEDICINE

Question/comment from a seeker:

There are many things that scare me. I have tried to overcome my fears with relaxation and mindfulness but it doesn't work because my mind is always in turmoil.

Seneca's answer (letter 50):

The weak and superficial mind is frightened by the unknown. Therefore, at first it will be necessary to try to redirect it again and put it back on the right track. Medicine is bitter to begin with, but when it bears fruit and heals us, it becomes sweet. Philosophy is equally sweet and healthy.

Psychological Reflection

Getting started with relaxation exercises always adds up. At first, it can be like wearing new shoes (which make you uncomfortable the first few times). But if you persevere, you will find that it pays to take care of your mental health.

The people who most need to learn to relax are often the ones who find it hardest (because they never relax). But we all have the ability to train our minds and control anxiety. Like everything in life, it is a matter of practice. Don't be discouraged, remember that the tortoise can beat the hare. You just have to walk slowly but surely, and with a clear goal.

73

WHO DOES NOT LIVE TO SERVE . . .

Question/comment from a seeker:

What about selfish people who only live for themselves? Sometimes they seem happier and more carefree than the rest.

Seneca's answer (letter 48):

One cannot be happy if one thinks only of oneself and seeks only to benefit oneself. Whoever wants to live for himself must also live for others.

Psychological Reflection

Although the Stoics preach not to be overly influenced by others and to go our own way, they also advocate universal human values such as friendship, kindness and helping as many as we can.

Seneca says that it is not possible to be happy by looking away from others and their needs. Happiness is related to our virtue.

We do not live alone; we are part of a whole. Mother Teresa once said: 'He who does not live to serve, does not deserve to live.'

74

NO ONE KNOWS YOU BETTER THAN YOU

Question/comment from a seeker:

People often tell me how to live my life and I get so overwhelmed. They think they know better than me what I should do and how I should feel.

Seneca's answer (letter 13):

Listen to yourself. Don't give too much importance to the words of others. Listen to your own feelings. No one can know you better than you know yourself.

Psychological Reflection

The fear of criticism and the obsessive need for recognition and 'likes' are a source of anxiety for many people.

When we always try to please others, we lose authenticity, spontaneity, creativity and sincerity—qualities that make us human. And we can reach the point where we no longer know what we want or what we like, developing an identity crisis.

Seneca recommends us not to give too much importance to the opinions of others and to calm this social anxiety, reminding yourself that no one knows you better than you do.

75

EXPERIENCE

Question/comment from a seeker:

Sometimes I act impulsively without thinking, and by the time I realise what I've done, it's too late, I've already messed up.

Seneca's answer (letter 68):

We should have reflected beforehand to realise that many things are unnecessary and absurd. But having failed to do so, we will now have to realise this through direct experience.

Psychological Reflection

In order to save ourselves a lot of trouble, it is better to think before we act. Deep down we already know what is good and bad for us. But sometimes it is necessary to experience things first in order to understand them properly.

As the Spanish proverb says: 'The devil knows more by being old than by being the devil.' The saying teaches us that the more experience we gather, the more we know.

When was the last time you learnt something from personal experience?

76

BEING SELF-DEMANDING

Question/comment from a seeker:

Why do human beings always want more and get so stressed about it?

Seneca's answer (letter 9):

Epicurus says: 'If you think that what you have is not enough, you will be unhappy even if you possess the whole world.'

How are you going to feel good if you are always dissatisfied with the situation you are in? Try to be grateful for your life—not just one day but every day.

The wise man is not affected by feelings of dissatisfaction because he appreciates what he has.

Psychological Reflection

Alan Watts, a British philosopher who brought Eastern philosophy to the Western audience, says that people don't know what they want and that this is for two reasons. One is that, in reality, what we want we already have. The second reason is that we do not know ourselves.

Following Watts' line, if we were more grateful for what we have, and spent more time on self-knowledge, we would have more clarity in our decision-making and greater inner peace.

Seneca agrees when he suggests that if we develop gratitude for what we have and are content with little, we will no longer demand so much of ourselves and will suffer less stress.

What do you want in life in terms of achievements or material things? On a scale of 0 to 10, how much stress and anxiety does that cause you? Is there a way you could be content without achieving that goal or having those material things?

77

THE BEST ATTITUDE

Question/comment from a seeker:

What attitude can help me in life?

Seneca's answer (letter 81):

We should be as grateful as possible. It is for our own benefit. Moreover, when you contribute to the benefit of others you also benefit yourself. And I am not saying this because they return the favour, but because the value of every virtue lies in being able to practise it, in being virtuous.

So let us avoid being ungrateful in order not to harm ourselves. And let us remember that in doing wrong to others, they receive the lighter portion of the harm. The worst part of evil always remains at home. The one who is really harmed by evil is the one who performs it.

Psychological Reflection

Seneca recommends us to have the mentality of grateful people. This attitude will help us to take the ups and downs of life with philosophy and optimism.

He also reminds us that our actions affect ourselves first and others second. If we do something wrong, it will weigh on our conscience. And the same applies for when someone harms us: the evil will stay mostly inside his or her 'house' (conscience).

78

DON'T DWELL ON IT ANYMORE

Question/comment from a seeker:

Sometimes I get obsessed with problems that have no solution.

Seneca's answer (letter 49):

Why do you get overwhelmed by the problem when the smart thing to do is not to dwell on it, instead of trying to solve it?

Psychological Reflection

Even philosophers, thoughtful people, tell us that sometimes it is better to accept that not everything can be fixed and that not every question has an answer.

If, in trying to solve a problem with all our efforts, we do not make progress, what is the point of continuing to think about it? Sometimes, time fixes everything.

Have you ever faced a problem that seemed to have no solution, but over time it solved itself?

79

HOW TO LIVE A GOOD LIFE

Question/comment from a seeker:

If you had one last piece of advice to give me, what would it be?

Seneca's answer (letter 123):

No one is good by chance; virtue requires practice and learning. To be driven by pleasure is immature and unevolved, common to animals and lower species. Success and fame are fleeting things, which change more than the wind. Economic resources are not the most important considerations.

Death is not a bad thing. It is the only law of life that makes all human beings equal.

Psychological Reflection:

What can you do to live in a way that is more aligned with this last piece of Seneca's advice?

BIBLIOGRAPHY

Séneca, L. A. (1984). *Cartas morales a Lucilio.* (English: *Moral Letters to Lucilius*). Volumen I-II. Barcelona: Ediciones Orbis, S.A.

Sèneca, L.A. (1929). *Lletres a Lucili.* (English: *Moral Letters to Lucilius*). Barcelona: Tipografía Emporium, S.A.

Séneca, L.A. (1915). *Obras escogidas de Séneca.* (English: *Selected Works of Seneca*). Paris: Garnier Hermanos.

Aurelio, M. (1985). *Meditaciones.* (English: *Meditations*), Madrid: Alianza Editorial S.A.

Burns, D.D. (2006). *Adiós, ansiedad.* (English: *When Panic Attacks*). Barcelona: Ediciones Paidós Ibérica, S.A.

Ellis, A. (2016). *Cómo controlar la ansiedad antes de que le controle a usted.* (English: *How To Control Your Anxiety Before It Controls You*). Barcelona: Ediciones Paidós Ibérica, S.A.

Fromm, E. (2003). *La atracción de la vida.* (English: *For the Love of Life*). Barcelona: Ediciones Paidós Ibérica, S.A.

Rosal, R. (2003). *¿Qué nos humaniza? ¿Qué nos deshumaniza?.* (English: *What Humanizes Us? What Dehumanizes Us?*). Bilbao: Editorial Desclée de Brouwer.

Séneca, L.A. (1986). *De la cólera.* (English: *On Anger*). Madrid: Alianza Editorial, S.A.